Passive Income

The Proven 10 Methods to Make Over 10k a Month in 90 Days

Table of Contents

Introduction

Do you envy the business people who constantly talk about how they have all the time in the world to go on vacation, and that they can afford these luxurious vacations? Have you often wondered how they did it?

If you ask them, you will most likely receive a vague answer that referred to some investments or passive income. But what is passive income?

Ideally, passive income is income that is relatively regular and comes from a source that you put minimal effort into every month to earn. This can be things like stocks or bonds, or it can be something like an eBook you wrote. This type of income can bring you anywhere from a few dollars a month if you don't work hard at it in the beginning, for well over ten thousand dollars a month if you put some effort into it in the first few months.

In this book, you're going to learn about ten different ways to make a passive income with very little investment when it comes to money. Once you earn some passive income off these methods, you can easily turn around and invest that money into other passive income methods that involve an initial investment. You see, it's a snowballing effect once you put in that initial effort!

But before you begin investing time, effort, and money into your passive income venture, you need to develop a new mindset. It's called the money mindset, and it will help you realize that you deserve the income you're going to gain!

Chapter One – The Money Mindset

Before you even begin to think about making over ten thousand dollars in a month in just ninety days, you have to know what the proper mindset is in order to achieve that goal. You see, your mindset is extremely important to what you want to achieve. If you tell yourself you can't do something, then you won't be able to achieve it! So let's explore how you can have the proper money mindset in order to get rich!

First, let's take a look at an example of someone who has a money mindset and someone who doesn't. We'll take a look at two handymen. Handyman one, let's call him George, walks into a home and he is approached by the homeowner. The homeowner tells him or her they want crown molding put in their upstairs bathroom. George affably agrees it will make the appearance of their home nicer, but that's it.

Now, the second handyman's name is Josh. Josh walks into the home and he approaches the homeowner who tells him about wanting the crown molding. Josh also agrees it will look nicer, but he also goes on to explain how the crown molding will improve the value of the home over the long run.

Do you see the difference? George just wanted to make the home look better for aesthetic purpose only, but Josh saw the *value* in putting the crown molding in from an investment standpoint.

Being able to see the value in something is the money mindset. There are numerous other aspects to the money mindset, so let's take a look at them.

#1 Mindful of the Long-Term

There are many people out there who are looking to make money fast, but they rarely ever make a lot of it because of greed. Their first mindset is to think about what's in it for them. Rather, they should be thinking about how they can add as much value to someone else first. For example, it's like building credits with someone or an organization over the long-term. You might never need to use those credits, but if you do, help is returned in abundance. Don't allow your short-term greed destroy your long-term wealth.

#2 You Deserve Only What You've Earned

There is no room for an attitude of entitlement for someone when they have a money mindset.

Don't expect to get to the corner office without paying your dues. At sixty-three years old, the man who put up the crown moldings is a great example of someone who doesn't expect something. He comes in with a good attitude to his job, does it well, cleans up, and leaves.

#3 You Believe You Deserve to be Wealthy

Money is out there for anyone to get their hands on. Once you believe you deserve to have that money, you'll subconsciously change your actions to make it happen. Stop feeling guilty about earning six figures in a year. There are people out there who earn seven and drive their companies into the ground to do it! Your mindset should not be 'why me' but 'why *not* me'? With the belief that you deserve to be wealthy too, your income will soar!

#4 You Ask Yourself What the Value of The Product or Service is Before You Spend a Dollar

People who have the money mindset are very value aware. Since they realize how hard it is to make money, they are much more careful about spending their money than the average person. They have to ask whether one dollar spent might return that dollar in the future. They are on the lookout for great deals and tend not to feel buyer's remorse because they purchase things that have a greater value than what they paid.

#5 You're Always Looking for Synergies and Leverage

When you go out to play tennis with people at a club or you're hanging out with some new friends, get excited! There could be synergies involved with those people. Not only are you having a good time with those people, but you are parlaying your relationship right into an excellent business opportunity. A website is an excellent example of leveraging assets to earn more. Besides earning advertising money, you can earn money by selling products and services. Your website can also serve as an online resume PR hub if you want to do more public works. If you haven't started a website, you really ought to!

#6 You Realize a Dollar Spent Today Could Grow To Much More In The Future

People who have the money mindset are naturally frugal. They despise letting go of too much money because they've already figured out what they spent today might have turned into if they had saved and invested at a ten percent rate of return over the following five to thirty years. Compound growth anchors money mindset people into spending less than they have earned. With an aggressive savings rate, you'll be surprised with just how much you could accumulate in a 401k in ten years.

#7 You're All About Tax Optimization

It's imperative to think about how much you have to earn before purchasing a particular item due to taxes. A car that costs $21,000 requires you to actually earn $30,000 in gross income. In terms of making money, someone who has a money mindset will look to reduce their taxes by figuring out the most tax friendly way they can make money passively, such as dividends. They also look to synergize their expenses if they are a freelancer or small business. There's no reason to do a company offsite in North Dakota if you can do one in Kauai. Figuring out how to pay little or no taxes becomes a hobby for someone with a money mindset.

#8 You Believe Excuses are No Excuse

You're either going to make it happen or you're going to fail. Failure is just fine; just don't make excuses and not do something about it. Figure out the reasons why you failed and then try again until you succeed. You need to believe you deserve only what you've earned, you take ownership for your failures and you most past them. Excuses are for those who blame the world for their shortcomings rather than themselves. The more excuses you use, the less you believe you are able to make things happen on your own.

#9 You Never Fail Due to a Lack of Effort

You can fail because your competition is incredibly talented, there was bad timing, or a natural disaster happened, but you will never fail due to a lack of doing your best. There are many people out there who say they are going to make a living writing or freelance programming, but most of them won't even send a draft of what they're writing to someone else for feedback. They don't want to put in the time to make the money.

#10 You Execute Solutions

Recognizing a problem or coming up with an idea is one thing. Coming up with the solution is more important. There are so many people out there who like to point out injustices or complain about something, but none of them doing anything about the situation. Someone with the money mindset will find a way to get it done and make it better.

If you read through this chapter and you believe you don't have the money mindset, don't despair! Anyone can develop the money mindset. The first step is to know you're worth it and believing that you deserve to be wealthy.

If you put in the effort, there is no reason you can't be enjoying that passive income flow, too.

Now that you know what the money mindset is and you know where you have to change in order to become wealthy with passive income let's look at the amazing ways you can make ten thousand dollars in a month in just ninety days!

Chapter Two – Making Money as a Coach

Are you currently struggling to make money with your coaching business but you have an expectation to make ten thousand dollars a month? Stop struggling! It's absolutely possible to make six figures a year coaching business, and it can happen pretty fast if you follow the necessary steps you need in order to fill your e-mail list and focus on getting more calls.

These are the top tips for making ten thousand dollars a month or more in as little as ninety days. That doesn't mean it's going to happen overnight easily. Building a business takes some focus and some effort. The goal is to build relationships and help the ideal client solve specific problems they're facing, and you're the coach and mentor that can help them with the problem.

The first step is developing that money mindset. Having the right mindset is extremely important when it comes to almost anything in your life. Making a consistent ten thousand dollars a month is not an exception.

You can create a vision board in order to visualize your goal. Just cut out some pictures and words from a favorite magazine and add them to a pinboard. You can also create an online one with Pinterest that's private and filled with inspiring images and quotes!

Once you've developed the mindset, you need to test those coaching packages.

Test the Packages

Market research is the core principle of making a thriving coaching package and coaching business. Don't make a package you believe will sell. Create a package based off what your ideal client actually desires.

In the first module of testing your packages, you need to ask detailed questions of your target market to be sure you are going to make packages that will actually sell. Don't skip this step! Make your market research your priority.

If you already have packages that are not selling, then find out why. Ask the ideal client what they would like to see added to the package or if there is anything else you can help them with. Change your copywriting in order to put an emphasis on the benefits and allow the readers know exactly what they can expect to occur if they work with you.

Price the Packages

In order to bring your income goals to life, you need to price your services and packages accordingly. Many coaches undercharge for their services. But if you want to be someone who goes to exotic locations and has financial freedom, then you need to create a premium coaching package!

Perhaps the thought of charging more for your package frightens you. If this is the case, keep working on your money mindset and remind yourself that your services are worth it for your clients.

Making a good income from what you do for a living will help you not only have a happy, healthy life, but it will help you be of a greater service to your clients. You'll have more income you can invest in your education as a coach, which will help you keep enhancing your skills.

Here are the following action steps you should follow in this section:

1. Figure out how many of your current coaching packages you have to sell in order for you to make the ten thousand dollars a month.

2. Ask yourself if you are undercharging. If you are, increase your rates and make new packages.

3. Work on your money mindset and beliefs if you are bumping against statements like *I can't charge that much*. It's not your packages that are the problem, it's you.

Lead Generation

Ads are an excellent way to generate leads. In fact, they're so important when it comes to growing a coaching business that they are one of the essential keys to financial freedom! Try some Facebook or Google ads for your coaching business and you'll see it increase.

There are other ways you can generate leads, too, such as going through a guest post, doing a webinar, joint ventures, and teleclasses. Whatever you choose to begin with, keeping going with it! Make sure to keep your efforts going so that your list grows with those are interested in getting to know you and the services you provide.

Here are the actions steps that will lead you to success!

1. Create some sort of lead generating strategy. How many leads to you require coming in so that you can hit ten thousand dollars a month? How many discovery or strategy sessions do you need to have to sign the number of clients you need in order to result in ten thousand dollars a month?

2. Invest time and learning in how to run Facebook ads or pay an expert to set them up for you.

3. Read and post on how to do a webinar.

4. Begin using Facebook ads or Google ads to promote your first webinar or opt-in gift.

Consistent Marketing

A successful coach will not flip-flop when it comes to their business. They will be consistent in marketing and expanding their reach. Ask yourself how consistent you are with marketing when it comes to your business. Are you in touch with your e-mail subscribers on a regular basis? What can your readers expect from a blog or newsletter? How do your readers feel about your brand and what are they learning from you?

Consistent marketing and lead generation helps you obtain more clients and hit your ten thousand dollar a month income. It's not rocket science. It's a formula that successful coaches and marketers have been following for some time.

Here are your action steps for continuous marketing.

1. Consider hiring a virtual assistant or hiring and intern for a few hours a week so you can focus on client generation activities.

2. Focus on some money making activities, such as getting leads, booking discovery calls, marketing, and much more. E-mail your list of contacts three times a week with one newsletter and two solo e-mails. Solo e-mails are the ones you send out that have a single call to action. It usually has something to do with income generation.

Be Consistent with Your Message

A successful coach will be reliable and consistent. They will tell the world exactly what they do, who they help, and how their clients can get in touch with them. Because they are so clear in their branding and message, people refer business to them. The media reaches out to them for expert commentary. Bloggers want to interview this coach, and joint venture partners come forward to ask if this person is interested in talking at an online telesummit.

What is it you want people to remember you for? Never be vague in what you do. If you're a life coach, then ask yourself the specific problems you want to help your clients with. Remember, you can always expand this, but in the beginning, you should be a specific as you can.

Here are some action steps to help you stay consistent with your message.

1. Read your past solo mailers, newsletters, and social media posts. Are you consistent with the message? Does your message make sense and is it compelling?

2. If you're not getting the discovery sessions, income, or clients you'd prefer, look over your marketing and ask yourself if you would buy your product. Is it inspiring you to take action?

Become Comfortable with Sales

In order to make ten thousand dollars a month being a coach, you have to become comfortable with sales and have sales conversations.

Most people have been brainwashed into believing sales is something that is unpleasant and sleazy, and it's not. When you are building your business as a coach, you're making packages for people who are interested in what you have to offer them. You're making helpful blog posts and newsletters that add value to the people you're serving.

So in other words, the people who are using our content are already interested in you and what you're doing.

Sales and marketing make people feel uncomfortable because they have had experiences in the past with products or messages that were deceptive. You're running a service-based business that is designed to help the people you are serving, and they want your help! There is a huge difference between spam messages and a well-crafted, very helpful newsletter from someone you want to hear from.

If you're still not sure about sales, know it will take some practice and consider learning more about how to do it. Keep working on the money mindset and you will realize you are an amazing asset to the world!

It's really as simple as that to make money as a coach. Find something you know is valuable to offer others, and then market it to those who want to listen. You will find clients in no time!

Chapter Three – Affiliate Sales

Making money online is excellent, but let's face it; most Internet marketers and bloggers are going to end up making very little money. When they are asked why they make so little, most are going to say they are a small site and they don't have enough traffic. Therefore, it's not shocking that a lot of the questions out there about how to make money with affiliate sales relate to how to obtain more traffic. It's possible to make money online with small traffic. What's more important is how you *monetize* that traffic.

Let's go over some of the pointers you need in order to make more money with an affiliate sales blog or website!

Do you make the maximum amount possible?

Most bloggers will monetize their blogs with some Google Ads or another advertising network. They might also do some affiliate marketing by recommending a book and linking to Amazon with an affiliate link. The problem with this business model is the payout is small. You're going to make five to twenty-five cents on a Google Ad click nineteen dollars from a thirty-seven dollar Clink Bank product, and just sixty cents if you link to a ten dollar book on amazon.

At those low rates, you have to sell a lot of volume to make a decent amount of money. Even at twenty-five cents a click, you need forty thousand clicks a month to make ten thousand dollars a month. Assuming two percent of your readers click on the ad, you need two million views just to make ten thousand dollars a month! There are very few blogs out there that make that sort of money.

Scale versus Magnitude

There are two ways you can increase your online affiliate earnings. You can increase the amount of traffic that comes to your site, this is scale, or you can make more money on the traffic you already have, which is magnitude. Most bloggers will put more of an effort to getting more traffic. If you're making a thousand dollars a month with a hundred thousand views, then you should make two thousand dollars with two hundred thousand views. That's the logic behind it, but is that really what will happen?

The reality is that most bloggers never achieve this scale in order to make a living online. The funny thing is that it's not the scale that is the problem. It's the magnitude. Most bloggers and Internet marketers are promoting small ticket items that make them pretty much nothing. What they need to do is go after the bigger ticket items.

Let's say you want to make ten thousand dollars a month and you have a choice of two different ways to do it. The first way is to sell a ten dollar eBook and the second way is to tell a ten thousand dollar mastermind. Which do you think will be the easier path to making ten thousand dollars a month? Selling ten thousand cBooks or selling one mastermind?

Of course, you'd much rather just sell one product rather than have to sell a thousand. If you want to make a large amount of money online off affiliate sales, you have to have high-ticket offerings in the product mix. Yes, it will take a little more effort to sell a ten thousand dollar product rather than a ten dollar product, but it won't be a thousand times more effort. It might take four to five times more effort.

When you try to sell high-end ticket items, it will take a personalized approach. You need to get on the phone with a lead and talk to them. This can take away from living that Dot Com lifestyle, and so the solution is to let someone else do it.

Stop banging your head against the wall in an attempt to achieve more scale. That's not your answer. The answer is magnitude of sales.

Adding Your High-Ticket Offer

There are two ways you can add a highly priced product to your marketing mix. The first way is to make it yourself. If you have never made a high-priced product before, then this isn't a great idea. The second way is to license a system such as MOBE and promote their suite of high-ticket products.

The nice thing about using MOBE is that you don't have to do the selling. They have a phone team that is experienced and will close the deal for you.

If you're interested in making your blog make more money for you while you sit back and enjoy a beverage on the beach, then look into affiliate sales!

Chapter Four – eBook Sales

EBooks are a popular way to attempt making passive income on the Internet; however, many underestimate just how difficult it is to market them properly. If you want to know how you can make ten thousand dollars a month off eBook sales within ninety days, then you need to read this chapter!

Step One: Put In the Work

You have to put in the time it takes to become an expert at something before you write an eBook on it, or you have to invest in a very talented ghostwriter who can write an eBook for you on the topic of your choice. You don't have to, but it is recommended that you know something about the topic you're trying to publish.

Step Two: Listen to the Market

If you are a professional in another industry or you want to write a specific eBook, you need to go out and do research on the market. Look at reviews on other eBooks before you write or have written the eBook you want to publish. What needs to be in it? What are people looking for? If you can tap into what they want in a book, you can market directly to them and many others who are in the crowd shouting the same thing.

People are not shy about what they do not like in a book, so listen to them.

Step Three: Write

Most agile writers who have been in the industry for quite some time can write a best seller in a month. Yes, a month! You have two months before you need to do advertising, so sit down and write every day just as if it were a full-time job. If you treat it as anything but a full-time job, you won't succeed.

Step Four: Solicit Feedback

This is probably one of the most important steps for writers. If you want a book that will reach high expectations and blow people's minds, you need to solicit feedback from those very same reviewers you saw on other books similar to your topic. Find their e-mail addresses and send them a brief explanation of what you need and why they should help you. Plead to their ego if you have to! You need their feedback no matter what.

Step Five: Listen to Your Beta Readers!

You need to listen to every piece of advice you get from your beta readers. In order to do this, you have to shift your mindset. Writers feel philosophical and feel they need to hold onto their artistic vision as much as they can. Your artistic philosophies are not what will make you money.

If your beta reader says a sentence doesn't make sense, then you need to change it. If they say they don't like the amount of words to explain a topic, then think about revising it. Your beta readers are there to help you, not there to boost your ego.

Step Six: Build Your Website

You need a website for your book or you won't generate sales. It has to look credible and legitimate, be built on a platform you can easily update or change, offer a shortcode so you can make content readable, have an e-commerce service, and allow you to fulfill orders for digital products.

Step Seven: Produce a Minimum Viable Product

To keep your cost low, you should make PDF versions of your eBooks available when you launch. Why should you do this? Because it's easy for readers to use and it's cheaper for you. You can read a PDF on any type of device, and you can make notes in it! Perfect for the reader who likes to highlight.

You can easily upload onto many other websites, too, such as Amazon and Barnes and Noble's Nook service. Once you do that, you need to find a professional to make a cover. The cover is one of the most important parts of the book other than the content. People *do* judge books by the cover, so make sure it's a good one!

Step Eight: Decide on Your Price

Pricing is imperative to success, but you want to do something that most people never think to do. Offer your book for a higher price than your competition. Why? Because people are naturally prone to believe that a product they pay more for is better than the competition, even if it's not! This is an age-old sales trick and it works every time.

For example, people will pay two dollars for an ice cream cone and say it was okay. They will then pay ten dollars for the same cone and the same ice cream and they will say it tastes better than the two dollar cone, even if it's the same exact cone and ice cream! It's a well-known phenomenon in the psychology world.

So if you want to sell more and earn more, then put your book at a higher price. After all, you put hard work into that book and you deserve to get a return on your investment! Stop short selling yourself.

Step Nine: Launch

Once you have everything set and in place, you need to launch. The first place you want to go for sales is your beta readers. Send them all an e-mail letting them know the book is published and they can buy it at several locations. Include links! You'd be shocked by how many of them will want to support you, because why not? You should have listed their names in the back with a huge thank you for all the effort they put into the book for you. Acknowledgment sections were not made for just any old reason.

Once your beta readers have boosted you to the top of the charts, start sending out emails to people who have bought similar books in the same genre. You can find their e-mail addresses on their profiles online on many different websites, such as Amazon.

Keep up with the feedback you get from people, tweak the book where it needs to be tweaked according to reviews and then sit back and watch as it makes you money month after month!

If books aren't your thing, then why not stock photography? Take a look at that in the next chapter!

Chapter Five – Stock Photography

It's said that no one can make money with stock photography. In this chapter, I'm going to tell you all about how to make ten thousand dollars *every month* within ninety days with your stock photography. It will take some work, but it will be well worth it in the end.

Step One: Equipment

In order to get started with great stock photography, you have to have the proper equipment. Your stock photography should not be taken with an iPhone. It should be taken with a high-quality, digital camera. You need a camera where you can control the settings, such as a digital SLR camera, over a point and shoot camera. Your camera has to be able to take sharp images.

Images submitted to certain websites are inspected by a person on the other end who approves the image before it can be posted. This means you need to take the time to learn the ins and the outs of your camera in order to take a technically correct image.

While the application process for some of the higher microstock photography sites can be more difficult, getting started with one of the hundreds of other microstock sites is an excellent platform. Don't feel dejected if you're rejected by the first photography site you apply to. There are plenty of others and you will improve with your camera in no time!

Step Two: Build Your Portfolio

Developing a robust and diverse portfolio is essential because selling microstock is definitely a numbers game. You should set a goal of how many photos you will upload on a monthly, weekly, or annual basis. You should start with two hundred images a month. You can scale back later when you're making more money.

You should get started with potential commercial uses for images and take advantage of any connections you have with another type of industry. If you know someone who has a bakery, ask them if you can take some photographs. If you know someone who has a beautiful garden, try getting some photos of that. Find something unique, like a pet shop that will let you take photographs of the various amphibians they have. It sets you apart as a photographer.

Look into the sphere of influence you have and see what you can find.

Remember that when it comes to stock photography, generic is the better option. There shouldn't be any recognizable brands in your photographs. Photos with properties and people will require a model or a property release to be signed before you can sell the photo.

Help improve your odds of selling your images by using the right keywords, too. Think of it as a Google search and all the ways people might look for your image. And don't forget you can also sell audio and video clips on microstock websites, too!

Step Three: Microstock Is Not the Only Way to Make Money Online with Photography

While microstock is an excellent way to start making money online with your photography, don't think of it as the end game! It's just the beginning so you can create a portfolio you can send to editors of online magazines and websites.

Just make sure the stock photography you shoot is something that you enjoy!

In the following chapter, you'll learn how to make money with movies and videos rather than still pictures!

Chapter Six – Make YouTube Videos

YouTube videos and channels are an excellent way to get traffic back go blogs and also a great way to obtain new followers. Unfortunately, due to some updates done by Google, it became harder for bloggers to obtain new followers and keep their old ones. But creating some YouTube videos will help you. These can bring in some serious advertising money and affiliate sales if you do it right.

Here's how you can use YouTube videos and channels to help you reach your income goals in just three months!

#1 Use It to Generate Traffic for a Website or Blog

If you have a blog that brings you income, then you need traffic. Many websites were hit hard by Google's updates on SEO and traffic, and if this happened to you, then you're probably hurting. You can use YouTube to not only get that traffic back but increase it! Get set up with a video camera or even use a camera on your laptop or tablet, and begin repurposing older content into videos. It's perfectly fine to have a video at the top of the blog post and the text underneath. There are people who enjoy reading posts and others who would much rather watch a video. Cater to both of them! Make sure you link to your website when you upload your video to YouTube, that way you can funnel the traffic to where you want to go.

#2 Create Products and Promote Them

If you're making your own products or you're providing a service, then YouTube offers some great ways to promote products and make sales. Products you can make are applications, eBooks, music, and art. Make your products, add them to a shopping cart, and then use YouTube to promote them. Add a link to the product in the description of the video so viewers can immediately go purchase the product.

#3 Sell Affiliate Products

Affiliate marketing is selling products in exchange for a commission. There are thousands of companies that offer attractive deals to an affiliate marketer who promotes their product, especially Amazon and eBay. In addition, you can join an affiliate network, such as Commission Junction, ClickBank, or ShareASale.com.

Once you're part of the affiliate program, review the affiliate products you're trying to sell online with a YouTube video and put the affiliate link in the video description area. Instead of reviewing, you could also do 'How To' tutorials. Once you make a video and upload it, you don't have to touch it again if you don't want to and the sales will keep coming in!

#4 Create a Web TV Series

Do you like telling stories? Then you could create your own television show on YouTube! You're only limited by your imagination and funds. You can make a drama series, comedy series, or even a talk show. Be aware that YouTube does limit your show's length to fifteen minutes; otherwise, you have pay for an increase in limit. But you can say and do a lot in fifteen minutes!

#5 Become a YouTube Personality

Stars on YouTube can make a very nice income. Some stars have almost a billion channel views, and at seven dollars per one thousand views, the income will soon mount up. If you have some quirky ideas or a television personality, then develop a YouTube channel. You might be the next YouTube star.

#6 Monetize With a YouTube Partner Program

After you've made several videos, it's time that you joined the YouTube Partner Program. All you have to do is enable the channel for monetization and you will receive a share of the income from advertising companies on

YouTube. Just as a YouTube star does, you'll be paid for every one thousand views on the videos.

#7 Share Knowledge and Tutorials

In ninety days, you can record up to 180 videos to put on YouTube with How To information and tutorials. If you enable your channel to have monetization and get sixty thousand views on those videos in a month, you can earn well over ten thousand dollars a month. The trick is to find something that people want to watch. Share knowledge you have learned about your career or about a hobby. People are always looking for videos on how to construct something or how to repair something. Get creative with it!

#8 Test-Market Products

YouTube is a great place for market research! You can discover whether your idea is going to be profitable or not by simply uploading a video. If your product needs funding, make some videos for a campaign on a fundraising website. The views and comments on the video tell you whether the idea is viable in its present form. The YouTube audience will even help you make it a viable product, so your efforts are funded and are successful.

#9 Become an Expert on Meta Data

Did you know that one hundred hours of video are uploaded onto YouTube every minute? This means there's a huge competition for attention on there. You have to do everything you can to ensure that your videos are found. Your video's metadata helps. Metadata is the information that you give about your videos.

The video's title, description, and tags will also index to your video. To maximize your presence in promotion, search, and suggested videos and ad-serving, be sure your metadata is well optimized.

Optimizing your videos for search engines makes the difference between a successful video and a failure.

#10 Build Your Brand with YouTube

You're a brand and you have power. YouTube will help amplify you no matter what you're doing or what your job is. YouTube helps you become known for your strengths and making money. Even if you don't have a clear idea of how you can make money on YouTube, get started with making videos about your interest. You might just stumble across a gold mine. People have turned their pets into YouTube stars!

#11 Turn Your Pet Into a Star

You don't have to become a singer to be a

YouTube star. If you're lucky, you can shoot a video of your pet that just goes viral. So keep the camera handy and if you see something

cute or funny, upload it and don't forget that Metadata. You never know who or what is going to be the next YouTube sensation!

Putting videos on YouTube and becoming successful is all about the Meta Data. You need to search for keywords that will optimize the views on your video. Just be sure those keywords actually pertain to the video, or you will get some angry viewers.

The next way to make passive income is to make an app, and you don't have to be a programmer to do it.

Chapter Seven – Make an App

There are many different ways to make applications and make money. You could make an application to promote an existing business or product, or you can make an app that's purely for entertainment and to make money from it. Once you decide what type of app you want to make, take a look at how you can make one.

Apps to Promote Existing Businesses

If you want your application to promote an existing business, the quickest way to get this done is to hire a local application development company to make the application for you. You don't have to learn much about the process. Just show them some applications you enjoy and bring along your photos, text, and videos that you want in the application. If you can, try to design it to be something that is useful for others. Apple has tightened up a lot and will not publish applications that are just marketing material. If you want the most possible downloads, set the app to free. Once it's live, tell all your current customers about it.

Apps For Making Money

If your main goal is to make money from the actual application, the application cannot be targeted just to one country. You are not going to make money if you make an application about the mountains of Scotland or pubs in Ireland. Steer away from making an application that is for a seasonal event. To maximize revenue, start small and use the first few applications you make as some hands-on education. Purchase some source code, reskin it through updating the graphics and publish it for under five hundred dollars.

The less you spend on the application, the more money you will make quicker. Ideally, you shouldn't spend more than five hundred dollars on an application. Researching what is currently popular by looking what's on the top charts will help reduce your risk and make your application one that is already proven tow work. Of course, the more work you do yourself, the more money you will save on developers.

What about iPhone or Android?

The Android devices and iPhone devices use different languages for their application platforms, so people will choose to develop for one of them at a time in order to keep their costs down. If you want to make money, then choose the iPhone. It will get more downloads and revenue than an Android device. However, if you believe Android fits your demographic better, then by all means, develop for them instead.

If you are making an application to promote a business, it's better to use Android instead of the Apple platform. There are not any reviews prior to it being published and the app will go live in about twenty minutes after it's been submitted.

Should it Be Free?

Pricing will work differently in each application category. Free is popular in the entertainment and games categories, especially with the Android devices. Unless it's a complex, niche application, the safest option is to make two versions. One of them is free and the other one is paid. See which one makes you the most money and then work from that point. To begin making money from a free application, start putting ad networks in the app. After a few months, when you're more up to speed, you can experiment with some in-application purchase and other monetization options.

If you're looking for the most downloads, make the application free.

What Kind Should You Make?

The best way to make money from the application is to know the demand in the market for the application before you begin to develop it. Go to the iTunes store on a daily basis to look for the top free, paid, and grossing applications in the categories you're interested in. Download the applications and play with them. Are people downloading the type of application you want to make? If they aren't, maybe put that idea aside for now and move on to another idea.

Games make the most money out of any other category out there. If you want to start your own application business, then games are probably the category to get into.

Should You Hire Someone or Use Your Own Knowledge?

If you want to start an application business, then you should start to learn about making applications. Learn the pitfalls and how the application market works. Learn from the success stories and what they did in order to get there. You can lose a lot of money in the beginning if you pay developers too much to make an application if you don't have the basic knowledge of what's involved and how much effort it takes.

Check out some developer blogs for insight and tips. Teach yourself how to reskin a game and integrate ads.

Hire a team of programmers to make one if you want to make an application for a business. Hiring locally is the easiest way and the most cost effective. Outsourcing has some challenges but it will come with a lower cost. You can go to freelance websites to put together your own team.

How Much Risk Should You Take?

Aim to make a portfolio of successful applications rather than putting all your energy into just one application. Keep the risk low and the prospects for success high. In the beginning, it's easier to make one large application from many small applications. You will learn as you go along with every application you publish so the quality of the applications will increase. You will make mistakes and you will learn some valuable lessons. So keep the costs low at the beginning to so you're not bankrupt at the end.

If you want to make a company that makes many applications, then you need to learn the basic coding skills yourself so you can save a lot of money. Aim to be profitable as fast as you can. It should be fourteen days after you've launched. Never spend six months working on getting an application perfect yourself. Get a small section of it done, and then upload it to the store right away.

Ship fast because customer feedback is valuable to you. The information you learn from going through the publishing process and confirming your choices as being correct allows you to make more educated choices in the future.

Common Concerns for Those Who Are Beginning

Many people are concerned because there are applications just like theirsin the store already. This is good news, actually. You can go to websites and type in the name of the application. If it's not in the top rankings for its category, then you saved yourself a lot of time and money and you have found out that the demand for that application is not as strong as you'd like.

If you still think your application is wonderful and you want to make it, then go ahead! What you need to do then is put it in the idea drawer. If it's is a great idea, you want to give it every chance for success. So for the following two months, plan to publish ten small applications. Source the internet, change the graphics, add some ads, and upload it yourself. After the two months, you'll be a lot more knowledgeable and profitable, so you can take out that idea and look at it again. If it looks good after you've been successful with other applications, then try it out!

If you don't have any money, you can't make an application. That's a huge misconception! It's still possible to make applications if you can't afford to purchase a foundation. The cheapest way is to get started with the machine you have at the moment. If you have an iPhone, build an iPhone application. If you have a computer or an Android device, make Android applications. You don't need to purchase a smartphone in the beginning. The software you use to make the application will come with a free phone simulator so that you can view the application on your computer. To build the application, open an account with an application builder. To publish the application, you'll need a developer's license, but they're under a hundred dollars for one. It's well worth the investment.

The third common concern is that you have an application idea but you don't want someone you hire to steal it. Don't say that to them! It's a little insulting to question someone's professionalism. Instead, tell them you have an idea for an entertainment or health based application and ask them if they have experience in it. You don't need to give out pertinent details in the interview process.

In order to do this right, there is some hard work involved and you will become addicted to the laptop. There's a steep learning curve, too, and you might not seem some friends for a while. But it's well worth it in the end if you stick with it.

If you're not into building apps, what about making a course online?

Chapter Eight – Make an Online Course

Professionals and students weigh in on the benefits versus the costs of traditional higher education against some more practical and affordable options online. The online education industry is ready to surpass a hundred billion dollars in the next year. But where will it go? How can you get a piece of that?

A large portion of the money will go to the instructors, the people who are creating educational content around their expertise.

In fact, many can make ten thousand dollars a month in just ninety days with one online course! You don't need any professional certifications, just your own experience in your industry.

Here are a few examples of what you could teach.

Application development is a very lucrative educational program at the moment. Just make sure you know how to do it and make some solid, useful content and market your courses on a few different sites. In addition to application development, you could try out some programming topics. If you find you can't get anyone to bite with the programs, then try allowing some people to take it for free in order to build up some positive feedback. Then sell it.

What Can You Teach?

The examples above were technical examples, but there is a wide variety of subject online available to teach about. Naturally, courses that have a well-defined outcome and help the student earn money is going to perform better, but that doesn't mean there's zero market for a non-technical subject.

Begin by making an inventory of your skills and your own experiences, especially if you've overcome a challenge or a struggle in the past. Odds are there are others who struggle with the same challenges.

For examples, if there is a specific software program you need to use for your occupation, maybe you could make a definitive guide for that software.

Test Ideas and Don't Be Afraid to Fail

After reading some crazy success stories, you might want to try your hand at making a course, too. However, the first one you make might not earn you a lot of money. But don't give up! Give teaching another shot. Take a look around at what you can do that's both technical and not technical, and determine what it is you are truly passionate about and good at. Make a course for that and you'll likely get some takers.

Once you have an idea, you should spend a month making the videos and the next month editing them. Then send them out to some colleagues and allow it to be given away for free to some people in order to gain feedback. This will tell you whether it will be a success or not.

Where Should you Host Your Course?

Once you have a topic and a course created that you believe will be a success, the next question is where you will host that course. How are customers going to find it?

Some people choose to host their videos on their own website. This means they have to configure video hosting, the general technical structure, and payment processing. These people are usually already familiar with programming, so it's not an issue for them.

You can choose to host your videos on an online education marketplace like Udemy, which has more than five million recorded pupils. Udemy makes it easy for teachers to get started and they handle the video hosting and payment processing for you. Instructors on Udemy get thousands of people to sign up for their classes in just a few months. Some of the top instructors on the site make a few million dollars a year, so it's well worth the effort of making a few hours' worth of video.

Now, that is where it gets a little tricky. Of course, sites like Udemy want and need to make a profit in order to keep running, but they also rely on some excellent instructors to make courses for their sites. The current royalty structure is set up so that if the student is delivered to your course through their site, they keep seventy-five percent of the income in some cases. If you bring the student to your site through an affiliate link, then you get to keep ninety-seven percent of the revenue. However, they have to sign up through your unique tracking link.

Don't Forget Marketing

The biggest mistake people make when they are making an online course is to believe that if they build it, the masses will buy it. Whether you host the course yourself or on a platform, you will still need to fuel the initial traction and enrollments to the courses!

The people who make a million dollars with their courses have a large e-mail list of potential customers they can reach. That means that if you want to launch a course this year, you should start thinking about the people you want to let know about it now.

One tactic that works well is to recruit people with high-profile affiliate partners. These are people who have large e-mail lists of their own. Develop friendships with them and create a special offer for their audiences so it turns into a win, win, win situation.

Just make sure the courses you decide to offer are ones that people will be interested in and that you are knowledgeable about. They will know and leave bad reviews if they are not successful after taking your courses. It will not be an easy income in the first ninety days or so, but after that, you'll be able to sit back and watch the cash come rolling in!

Perhaps filming yourself and putting it online is not your thing, and that's okay! You can dry out something like drop shipping instead.

Chapter Nine – Drop Shipping and FBA

The idea is for those who want to make some serious passive income online. There is some work upfront and by comparison to some of the other ideas in this book, there is a fair amount of work on an ongoing basis. However, if you automate as much as you can with a virtual assistant, you can get it down to a few hours a week!

Drop Shipping

The idea for drop shipping is to find a product or a group of products that people have a hard time purchasing locally. Anything in niche hobby categories will work out well. It has to be something that isn't as easy to buy online, too. Then set up an online store.

Come to an agreement with a company directly and you have yourself set! When you have the agreement made with the manufacturing company, you then set up an online store where people can purchase the product. The order is sent to you, and then you send the order to the manufacturer. Then you can have the package delivered to you and send the order to the customer, or you can have the order sent directly to the customer.

There are a few things that can cause a problem with sending it directly to the customer. First and foremost, if there is a problem with the product, the customer will be upset. You can circumvent this by ordering the product and checking it out yourself before sending it to the customer. Second, if the customer finds out, they might try to buy directly from the manufacturer, too. You can keep that from happening by packaging the product with your own label and information. Most manufacturers will make products with your logos on them and information on them for you at an extra cost.

Drop shipping involves companies such as Alibaba, where you contact manufacturers of products directly and sign agreements with them for a certain amount of product. There are a few things you want to keep in mind before you sign an agreement and release the funds.

First, you want to make sure you can order one of the products in order to test it out and see if it's something you want to sell. Do this with every product! You need to know what you're getting and what you're selling to customers so that you can market it appropriately and make sure it's something worth paying for.

Second, make sure you're working with a well-known company. Remember, these companies are in different countries and there isn't much you can do once you hand over the money except know by their reputation that they will deliver the product on time.

Drop shipping is a lucrative business if it's done properly.

Amazon FBA

Fulfillment by Amazon is relatively easy to get set up and manage. While it's not completely passive, if you manage it right, you can make much more than ten thousand dollars a month.

The first step to making money with Fulfillment by Amazon is to find a product you believe will sell from a reputable manufacturer. Again, this is where Alibaba comes in. You can go to their site and look at popular items that people purchase for drop shipping or for Amazon's FBA program, and then you can go to Amazon to see how well those items are selling.

If you want to make a profit on the products you're selling, there are a few things to keep in mind.

1. Always make sure the product description is accurate and to the point. People want to know as much as they can about a product in as little words as possible.

2. Be prepared for negative feedback. Someone is going to get something they don't like or might be broken and you need to handle it in a professional manner. The best way to do this is send them a message privately if you can, and tell them how sorry you are about their bad experience. Then offer to refund their money in return for the broken product or to send them a new product that is not damaged. Apologize again, and never ask them to change their feedback! Most people will go back and change their feedback after the problem has been resolved. If it's not resolvable, move on and don't poke the bee's nest.

3. Don't limit yourself to products that sell at a high price! Many successful FBA members make a lot of money on small

products they don't have to spend a lot of money having shipped.

Amazon FBA is an amazing way to make money online! You just have to be smart about timing and know how to markup your product in order to maximize profit and sales at the same time. Do some research on the market you want to get into before you dive into it.

If you have some extra cash lying around from some successful ventures already, then you might want to consider what's in the following chapter.

Chapter Ten – Peer to Peer Lending

Peer to peer lending is exactly what it sounds like. You put money into an online account and then it's divided up amongst dozens to hundreds of people who are looking for loans. You will only be one of a few hundred other people lending that person money. So if they ask for a thousand dollars, you might lend them twenty-five dollars.

There are some things to keep in mind about this method. First, it is a little risky considering loans can go bad and this is technically investing. Second, if you choose to lend out only to people who have a high credit score, you get less of a return.

Here are some statistics from LendingClub.com, one of the most popular peer to peer lending websites out there.

First, the average FICO score of a borrower on LendingClub is 699. This is very good! The average person on LendingClub will have a sixteen-year credit history and they are of the top ten percent of the United States when it comes to their income. The average personal income of someone on LendingClub looking to borrow money is around seventy-five thousand dollars. In addition, the average loan size is fourteen thousand dollars.

Grade A loans will receive 5.26% annual return. Grade B loans receive 7.33%, and Grade C receives 8.69%. Now, keep in mind that Grade A loans are low-risk, meaning they are the most likely to be paid, so you receive less money with those. However, Grade C loans are high risk and you might end up losing some of the money you lent out.

Let's look at an example of how much money you might make if you were to loan out $100,000. If you loaned out to only Grade C borrower and you made 6% on that loan annually, and it was a thirty-six-month loan, you would make an average of just over three thousand dollars a month. Then, you could reinvest that three thousand dollars and boost your income even more!

Peer to peer lending is something you want to look into if you have some extra money you can invest, rather than investing your life savings. Earn some money with some of the other methods in this book, and then look into investing in those who are around you. You can help out others who need to boost their credit and you can line your pockets at the same time!

If peer to peer lending is not for you, then buying and selling domain names might be something you're more interested in.

Chapter Eleven – Buy and Sell Domain Names

Do you have a knack for knowing if a keyword will be popular or not? Then you might want to look into the sale of domain names! There are a few different types of domain speculation.

Domain speculation is knowing how to judge the value of a domain name. For most businesses and individuals, the practice is a full-time, profitable job.

There are two main types of domain speculators. There are the ones who purchase domains, build sites on them, and then flip the domain and the website. Then there are those who buy and sell the names without a site attached. While both of them are a lucrative business, the second type is easier for a beginner to learn.

How to Purchase Valuable Domain Names

Purchasing a domain name is easy, but finding one that will give you a profit is a little more difficult. There are many factors that determine if a domain name is valuable or not, but the major ones are memorability and SEO optimization.

One of the best ways to find a valuable domain is to purchase it via a domain auction site. The strategy is beneficial two different ways. First, any domain that has been purchased will most likely be researched again. Secondly, many of the recently expired domains still have some SEO attributes that were built up by the owner. For example, a recently expired domain name might have the backlinks on the web and the page rank of the domain might still be high, giving the purchaser instant SEO results with very little effort.

Using the keyword research tools is another excellent method for finding out which domains might prove to be valuable, as many webmasters use these tools when they're deciding what domains to purchase. If you obtain a domain name that has a popular keyword, then you can easily find a buyer.

Selling Your Domain Name

Obtaining what you think is a valuable domain name is the easy part of the task. Finding the right buyer is harder. Using auction sites and forums is most likely to the best method for finding a qualified buyer interested in your domain, and using an auction takes away some of the stress for establishing value.

If the domain name is already related to a certain niche, then you might find some success advertising in forums related to it. Just put a link in the signatures of the posts you make and speed up the selling process exponentially. While it might be possible to find a prospective webmaster on a niche-specific forum, it's generally better to advertise on a webmaster forum where there is a higher amount of potential customers.

Most auction sites have heavy amounts of competition and many of the domains for sale will include a pre-constructed website that might already generate a profit. Before you list your domain for sale, it's important to ensure you're not stepping into a market saturated with full websites and domain packages.

Squatting and Volume Selling

Unfortunately, most domain names are going to take a few months to sell, especially when they do not have a website attached to them. Therefore, there isn't a need to become discouraged if your name doesn't sell immediately. Most people will make the mistake of quitting their speculation endeavor after they wait a few months and don't have success. In reality, domain squatting is just as profitable and is a valid form of investing long-term.

Consider the domain name hammocks.com. How much was it worth in 1995, and then in 2010? For the domain owner who has patience, it sold for seven hundred thousand dollars in 2010. Rather than focusing on one, try selling a large volume over a long period of time. Remember, if you follow the principle of the domain name speculation, there's a good chance it will sell eventually.

Put a site on it with relevant information and SEO keywords, and it will sell even quicker!

Conclusion

Countless methods to make ten thousand dollars a month after ninety days of work have been discussed in this novel. You have to choose the one that sings to you the most. Are you a writer who wants to sell an eBook? Then you need to write the book and find the appropriate avenues for advertising. If you're a programmer who knows how to make applications, then start out with a few small ones that are free and add some advertising if and when they get popular. It's all about playing to your strengths and finding something that takes a short time of heavy effort with a long-term profit that takes minimal effort.

Stick it out for ninety days and work hard, and then sit back and enjoy the income. If you do this once a year, you can boost your income way above ten thousand dollars a month. Many people who have done two of these ideas at once, such as making a book about how to do something and then making instructional courses online make millions of dollars a year.

The sky is the limit! Remember to work on your money mentality, and then get started on your new business venture!

I hope you enjoyed the information you found in this book. If you did, please leave a review to let others know how they can enjoy the benefits.

Thank you for reading!

BEFORE YOU GO

If you liked this book you may like these other books from Mark Thomas

Check out more books by Mark Thomas

Free Bonus

As Promised Here Is Your Guide To
Creating More Hours In Your Day:
Discover How To Fit 48 Hours Of Work
In A Day

GET YOUR FREE COPY

LEARN HOW TO GET MORE DONE IN A DAY

Do you feel stuck, stressed, and pissed because you aren't able to get all of your most important tasks done in a day? Perhaps this book can be the answer to your struggles. Learn the ways to manage your time to get more things done in a day and free up time do things you enjoy in life. Procrastination and Distractions are the biggest enemy of time management. This book will teach

you the exact strategies to conquer
procrastination.

 Download "The Clockwork Course" For
FREE

If You Want Free Best Selling Kindle Books Delivered Straight To Your Inbox

JOIN OUR FREE KINDLE BOOK CLUB!

BE PART OF THE CLUB

Chapter 1

Why should you practice yoga?

Well, the first answer that pops out of the mouth of many yoga practitioners is –"Better health." According to the late yoga guru B.K.S. Iyengar, *"Healthy plants and trees yield abundant flowers and fruits. Similarly, from a healthy person, smiles and happiness shine forth like the rays of the sun."*

While this is 100% true, what we forget is that yoga works on your body-mind connection. *"I have been a seeker and I still am, but I stopped asking the books and the stars. I started listening to the teaching of my Soul."*

Thus goes the words of Jalāl ad-Dīn Muhammad Rūmī, the world famous poet and scholar. And, if you take a close look at these simple words, you will identify that yoga is the best and perhaps, the most natural way to start listening to your Soul. Yes, when you start listening to your mind, your physical health will be restored to its natural state.

Countless researches conducted on the impact of yoga pertaining to health prove that regular practice of yoga could help manage or control a wide array of health conditions.

Yoga

- ➢ Boosts your flexibility, strength, structural alignment, muscle tone, and stamina

- ➢ Eases tension, stress, nervousness, and anxiety

- ➢ Boosts self-confidence and self-esteem

- ➢ Enhances creativity, memory, focus, and concentration

- ➢ Helps in shedding the excess weight

- ➢ Improves circulation

- ➢ Improves the functioning of digestive system

- ➢ Stimulates your immune system

- ➢ Improves mental steadiness

- ➢ Inculcates a sense of peace, calm, and well-being

Now that you know why you should do yoga, can we move on to take a look at how yoga helps in healing your body and mind?

Chapter 2

Yoga as a cure for body and mind 'dis-eases'

Life, today, is complex, clogged with stress, tension, and anxiety. No one has time for oneself. It is always a hectic life which does not have any meaning. The result – your tummy starts popping out, your hips turn stiff, your wrists fight to move as it should, and not to forget the nagging headache.

And, we rush to the doctors and pop in some pills to ease these conditions. There is a shortcut for every ailment now. There are countless tricks out there that seem to be working on everyone but not on you, right? Well, it is now time to take a break from all those so-called 'magic' solutions.

Try yoga! Yoga encourages you to travel to a destination where there is nothing, except good and purity. No one is bad or nothing is wrong here. And, don't worry about twisting and tweaking your body into those pretzel-like postures. Ok, I do agree that yoga does have some complicated postures, but those are meant for the advanced practitioners, which you could also become with regular and dedicated practice. Till then, take it easy. All you need to do yoga is to know how to inhale and exhale consciously.

Said that, we will now just briefly take a few steps down to see how yoga helps in healing your body and mind.

Yoga and weight loss

Asanas, or the physical postures, we practice in Yoga work on various body systems, enticing and coaxing them to return to their actual functional mode. When your circulation improves, your digestion enhances. When your digestion is on track, your toxins are eliminated properly and naturally. A toxin-free body is metabolically active, which in turn, burns the excess calories stored. When the stored-up fat is used to produce energy, you will find yourself fitting into smaller sizes.

On a mental level, it eases the stress and helps you become more aware of what you eat. You will find yourself eating less. When you eat less, as I said, the body starts using up the reserves, promoting weight loss. Bonus – your cortisol levels come down, which is beneficial for shedding the excess pounds.

Yoga for stress and anxiety

Various yoga postures when practiced along with a breathing and meditation sequence teaches you to regulate your breath and relax your mind and body, when you come under the attack of stress and anxiety. These techniques flood all the body parts and brain with a fresh dose of blood, oxygen, and nutrients, setting the stage for overall peace and relaxation.

Yoga and self-esteem

Yoga makes you aware of your strengths and limitations. It strengthens your mind, enabling you to think and act better during crises. It corrects your posture, which quite often gets hampered due to lack of confidence and low self-esteem.

Talking in terms of Chakras or the energy centers of the body, various yoga postures help in activating the Manipura or Solar Plexus chakra, which is the center of self-esteem. A balanced Solar Plexus is what makes you accept your true self unconditionally.

So, are you ready to uncover the treasures that are hidden within you?

Fasten your seat belts.... And, here we go...

<u>Check out more books by Mark Thomas</u>

Thank you again for downloading this book!

If you enjoyed this book, then I'd like to ask you for a favor, would you be kind enough to leave a review for this book on Amazon? It'd be greatly appreciated!

Thank you and good luck! ☺

-Mark Thomas

www.ingramcontent.com/pod-product-compliance
Lightning Source LLC
Chambersburg PA
CBHW060407190526
45169CB00002B/796